AMONG THE GODDESSES

POETRY
  Spells
  Such Husks
  Calendars
  The Complete Poetry of Louise Labé (Translation)
  Eve
  The Encyclopedia of Scotland

PROSE
  A Poet's Ear
  A Poet's Craft
  The Body of Poetry
  The Ghost of Meter

EDITOR
  Multiformalisms
  Lofty Dogmas: Poets on Poetry
  An Exaltation of Forms
  Perspectives on Carolyn Kizer
  After New Formalism
  A Formal Feeling Comes

AMONG THE GODDESSES

An Epic Libretto in Seven Dreams

ANNIE FINCH

 Red Hen Press | *Pasadena, CA*

Book layout by Sydney Nichols

Library of Congress Cataloging-in-Publication Data

Finch, Annie, 1956–
  Among the goddesses : an epic libretto in seven dreams / Annie Finch.
— 1st ed.
    p. cm.
  ISBN 978-1-59709-161-9
  I. Title.
  PS3556.I448A8 2010
  813'.54—dc22

                        2010007836

The Annenberg Foundation, the James Irvine Foundation, the Los Angeles County Arts Commission, and the National Endowment for the Arts partially support Red Hen Press.

First Edition

Published by Red Hen Press
Pasadena, CA
www.redhen.org

Acknowledgements

Dedicated to my teachers and healers, more than can be named here, with gratitude for keeping me inspired and spiralling during this book's 17-year birth: Paula Gunn Allen, Annegret Baier, Cathleen Bailey, Jennifer Barrett, Jean Shinoda Bolen, Lisa Bowie, Glen Brand, Julian Brand, Z. Budapest, Jeanne Cameron, Janine Canan, Carol Christ, Jane Clow, Francesca de Grandis, Jack Fertig, Chas Finch, Dabney Finch, Henry L. Finch, Julie Finch, Margaret Rockwell Finch, Marta Rijn Finch, Roy Finch, Althea Finch-Brand, Marija Gimbutas, Andrea Goodman, Judy Grahn, Joy Harjo, Lynn Hueffed, Denise Jasmine, Michelle Jean, Cait Johnson, Betz King, Susie Landau, Gretchen Lawlor, Jennifer Lunden, Jean Liedloff, Erica Linen, Laurie McCammon, Sharon McErland, Patricia Monaghan, Pat Mora, Ajit Mookerjee, D.G. Nanouk Okpik, Oloye Aina Olomo, Jan Perkins, Abby Power, Marjorie Hughan Rockwell, Sonia Sanchez, Robert Schoenbrun, Ntozake Shange, Eileen Showalter, Lisa Siders, Starhawk, Suzanne Stevens, Merlin Stone, Kristina Sturiano, Kathleen Sweeney, Deborah Knighton Tallerico, Fred Tietjen, Marie Truscott, Turtle Woman, Anne Waldman, Alice Walker, Barbara Walker, Susun Weed, Sharon Wilke, and Alice Woodman.

Special thanks to Deborah Drattell for insightful suggestions about the libretto, and to Margot Adler for a comment that sparked the idea of interweaving the two versions. Gratitude to Kate Gale for loving the manuscript, Mark Cull for his design brilliance and patience, and all the good people at Red Hen Press for their care in making this book.

Books 6–8 of "Marie Moving," as well as part of the preface under the title "Writing Marie Moving," were published in slightly different form in *Thirteenth Moon*, Spring 2001. A section of Book 8, "Kali," appeared in *Rattapallax*, Spring 2007.

Contents

PREFACE

This book began in the late 1980s, as the women's spirituality movement was shifting the foundations of my psyche and with them, my poetics. It was conceived as an epic, spiralling out from the "Isis" chant. Though I completed most of the poem before I had an abortion in 1999, abortion was the climax of the plot from the beginning, as Demeter, Kali, and Inanna provide different perspectives that help Marie take responsibility for the implications of her choice in a spiritual context. The theme of abortion had long seemed to me an epic one, focusing a terrain of crucial energies and reclaiming the spiritual implications of women's inherent power over life and death.

I had written the series of goddess poems in my first book, *Eve*, and the epic, which I called "Marie Moving," was a natural next step. The poem's structure honored nine as the number of the goddess, with nine books of nine stanzas of nine lines each (the ninth book was omitted later). I chose the dactylic meter, which I had not written in before at length, not because it was the meter of ancient tales, but to evoke the rhythm of ocean waves and the depths of female power.

This book is "Marie Moving's" final version, interlacing the epic with a dramatic version of the same story written for composer Deborah Drattell in 2002. The libretto fused poetry, music, and dance to enact Lily's descent and archetypal encounters. In the process, the epic poem found the additional layers I had sought, and regained its ending. When Lily, part of a community at last, holds her baby up to the moon, the forces that have brought her to that place of peace and triumph have been articulated in music and silence as much as in language.

Among the Goddesses is printed in two typefaces so it can be read in three different ways. The blocky typeface on the far left yields the original epic narrative poem, "Marie Moving." The righthand typeface provides the libretto adaptation, "Lily Among the Goddesses"—a script for musical or dramatic performance. Reading the book straight through, as is my intention for the general reader, offers the reader the complete "epic libretto" that spirals between the narrative and dramatic layers of the story.

Annie Finch
Portland, Maine
April 2009

*Queen Anne's Lace seeds were a widespread and effective method of birth control among Native Americans, but, as I learned from herbalist Susun Weed many years after finishing Book 8, they are not an abortifacent. Black cohosh would have been an effective herbal abortifacent, but would have required longer to work than the three days described in the poem. I have exercised poetic license in keeping the story of the abortion the way it was when the poem was finished.

Manuscript page from the score for
"Lily Among the Goddesses"
music by Deborah Drattell

"LILY AMONG THE GODDESSES"
CHARACTERS

LILY/MARIE: A young contemporary woman.

KOURETES: A chorus comprised of three priests and/or priestesses of the Goddess.

EVE: An aged artist.

ISIS: The most famous Egyptian goddess, worshipped for thousands of years all over the Meditteranean. She was the sister and wife of Osiris (the constellation now known as Orion) and the mother of the god Horus. When Osiris was torn apart by his jealous brother in her absence, Isis travelled all over Egypt to find the pieces of his body and magically reassemble them. A powerful goddess of fertility and magic, she was also responsible for the invention of language. Here she is ten years old, with bare feet, many jangly bangles on her arms, a headdress of mirrors flanked by snakes.

ASTARTE: Very ancient Semitic goddess of fertility and war. Her earliest altars were stones and she was honored by the planting of trees. Here she is a column of rosy sandstone, perhaps with carvings.

RIGHTEOUS MAN: He is as archetypal as the goddesses, driven by the fury of his fear and his need for control.

DIANA: Roman name for the Greek goddess Artemis, Goddess of the hunt, of wild animals, of the moon, of chastity, and also of childbirth. Here she is a strong young woman in jeans and a backpack.

HECATE: The Greek goddess of the Underworld from 700 BC till late Antiquity. She was the goddess of crossroads and or doorways, of death and birth. In some myths she is the crone, a dark or waning aspect of the moon, forming a female trinity with Artemis (the maiden or new moon) and Selene (the mother or full moon). Here she is an old woman wearing a rusty black cape.

DEMETER: Greek goddess of fertility and the earth, who made all the crops grow (the word "cereal" comes from her Roman name, Ceres). In the myth that formed the basis of the Eleusinian Mysteries, Demeter's beloved daughter Persephone was abducted by Hades, the god of the underworld. Demeter searched for Persephone, so grief-stricken that all the earth's crops died. Finally, Zeus intervened, and arranged for Persephone to be with her mother for half the year and in the underworld for half the year, causing the seasons of summer and winter.

KALI: The fierce Hindu goddess of death and life. Here she is a weaver, short and frail, a mysterious figure who keeps her own counsel and answers to no one.

INANNA: The subject of the most ancient written poems in existence, she was worshipped for 3500 years as "Queen of Heaven and Earth" in ancient Sumer. The story of her death—for three days and nights—and her rebirth is recounted in hymns, stories, and carvings and made an epic poem in Wolkenstein and Kramer's *The Descent of Inanna*. Here she is an archaic statue, tall, stiff, and imposing, with eyes of blue stone.

"Lily Among the Goddesses"
Synopsis

Prologue

Lily, a young woman who has been traveling alone since she left her home as a victim of incest, invokes the blessings of women's traditions on her story. Surrounded by figures of goddesses, Lily sings about beginnings and endings with a chorus of three Kouretes (ancient priests of the Goddess). The Kouretes will take various roles to comment on the action throughout the opera.

Act I

Eve, a vibrant ninety-year old stained-glass artist, sits on the porch of her small house by the ocean, sketching. Around her are stained glass windows she has made in traditional goddess designs. Lily appears on the road passing the house. Eve invites Lily to have tea, and their friendship grows as they discuss their lives. Since Lily has no place to go, Eve invites her to rent the spare room. Lily moves in and becomes Eve's apprentice, helping her find stained glass. Through this friendship she develops a new trust in the significance of her life.

After several years, Eve dies and Lily walks alone on the beach at sunset, distraught. Returning home, she finds the goddess Isis in the form of a young girl sitting on her porch. Awed by this visionary experience, Lily serves Isis a meal and then takes her to the shore where she disappears among the stars to continue her mythic journey to her brother Osiris. Awakened into consciousness of the other dimensions of her life, Lily returns to the house and discovers another manifestation of female power which will change her life: the goddess Astarte in the form of a sacred pillar of stone.

ACT II

When Lily wakes the next morning a circle of trees—in ancient times planted as altars to the goddess Astarte—has grown around the stone. Singing her amazement and gratitude, Lily decides to go on a journey, planting the trees up and down the west coast in tribute.

Eight nights into Lily's trip, she is sleeping in a dark churchyard while the Kouretes sing with foreboding. A strange man comes into the churchyard while Lily sleeps, rummages through her possessions and, finding goddess symbols and candles, decides angrily that she is a "witch." In a rage of insane righteousness, and in spite of Lily's violent struggles, he rips her clothes and rapes her, finally retreating and running away after she manages to break one of his fingers.

Crushed with grief and anger, Lily pulls herself together and decides to travel to San Francisco to plant the last tree, since Eve has given her the name of her friend Diana, owner of the Café Artemis in San Francisco. Lily hitchhikes to the city where, in a crowd of people, she suddenly sees the terrifying figure of Hecate, goddess of crossroads and transitions. Prompted by this encounter into a shock of realization, Lily looks into herself and understands that the rape has made her pregnant.

In a shocked trance, Lily enters the Café Artemis, sits down, and sings a soliloquy on the tragic injustice of her situation. As she finishes, one of the Kouretes in the dress of a waiter introduces her to Diana. Finding a friend in Diana, Lily pours out her story. Diana helps Lily to plant the last tree and supports her in her decision to take the next stage of her journey, visiting Eve's old friend Demeter in Ohio.

ACT III

After a long bus journey, Lily arrives at the house of the prehistoric earth goddess Demeter and finds her in the garden. Lily is awed by Demeter's balanced strength and power. As Demeter sings about the earth and her own role as bringer of both death and life, Lily understands that she does not want to carry her pregnancy. On Demeter's advice, Lily travels to obtain the help of the Hindu war-goddess Kali in aborting the child.

Lily steps off a bus on a rainy night and approaches Kali's house. Through a window, she sees Kali weaving a magical tapestry depicting every form of life on earth. Kali opens the door at Lily's knock, but looks right past Lily and shuts the door in her face. Lily summons her deepest will as she knocks on the door again and, with all her power, insists that Kali let her in.

Inside the house, Kali opens a cupboard and mixes together a potion for Lily. Lily drinks it and enters a dark room lined with rows and rows of different goddesses, where she will spend three days aborting her baby. Most predominant is a large sculpture of the Meditteranean goddess Inanna, who spent three days in the underworld before she was resurrected.

In this room, Lily has a vision of Inanna's sister Ereshkigal focusing death through her body as the baby is aborted to the chants of the Kouretes and Kali. Newly aware of the gravity and sacredness of her body's power to give death and life, and of the balance between life and death in the universe, Lily leaves the room. In a final symbol of acceptance, the moon, ancient symbol of the female cycles of life, shines above a bare-branched tree.

Epilogue

Years later, Lily has moved to another part of the country and had a baby. On a quiet night, she stands near an ancient tree with a group of women and a few children. As the moon rises, she shows her baby, whom she has named Eve, the moon.

"Isis, Astarte, Diana, Hecate, Demeter, Kali, Inanna. . . ."
—Ritual Chant

Invocation

One plume of salt-spray thrown up by a rock-face,
one pebble left on the shore where it lands.
There is no end if there was no beginning,
so help me to tell where this ending began,
gathering women who touch, who honor,
who loom traditions through the body of earth.
Please lend me your voices, and some of our stories,
to spiral this shell through the layers of sand.
When it began, I was travelling in Oregon—

PROLOGUE

KOURETES *at stage front. Seven goddesses (*ISIS, ASTARTE, DIANA, HECATE, DEMETER, KALI, INANNA*) placed around the stage.* LILY *in the center of the stage starts a chant and weaves in and out of* KOURETES *and goddesses as* KOURETES *pick up her words.*

LILY:
> One pebble left on the shore where it lands,
> one plume of salt-spray thrown up by a rock-face,

KOURETES:
> one plume of salt-spray thrown up by a rock-face,
> there is no end if there was no beginning.

LILY:
> There is no end if there was no beginning.
> One plume of salt-spray thrown up by a rock-face,

KOURETES:
> One plume of salt-spray thrown up by a rock-face,
> one pebble left on the shore where it lands . . .

A winding road of light appears, leading towards a small house in the distance. LILY *begins to walk on it.*

LILY:
> Gathering women who touch, who honor,
> who loom traditions through the body of earth,
> there is no end if there was no beginning,
> so help me to tell where this ending began,
> gathering women who touch, who honor,
> who loom traditions through the body of earth.

KOURETES:
> Please lend me your voices, and some of your stories,
> to spiral this shell through the layers of sand.

LILY:

> to spiral this shell through the layers of sand.
> When it began, I was travelling onward. . . .

KOURETES:

> When it began, she was travelling onward . . .

Fade Out

BOOK 1: OREGON

—Searching the shore for the way to the beach,
I stumbled on Eve's small weathered house.
Out on the porch where the fog had come rolling
past in the morning leaving mist on the railings,
she drew charcoal patterns of spirals and bird-wings
while her deep-coiled braids gleamed bright in the sun.
"Good morning," I called, past the pile of stained glass,
and Brigid, my black dog, bounded up towards her.
Eve spoke to her easily, quickly; I saw

Brigid's eyes gleam yellow as she recognized her,
and my heart beat faster. Eve invited me in.
In green wicker rockers, we talked several hours,
while Brigid slept stretched at our feet. And we learned
why I had left home, why she had stayed here,
how her long-ago story still colored her days,
how I hoped to find safety with people again.
She laughed with me easily, bracing her foot
on a wide, dark-whorled railing, retracing a circle

with one wrinkled toe. When she reached for the tea
I saw her eyes leapt like quick fish. I felt fire.
Her two hands vibrated with so many lines
they were conscious with age. They rested free of each other.
She had lived here for decades, in four small white rooms,
awakened by shore. She asked me to stay.
Because no-one had heard me like this yet, I stayed.
I rented her spare room—a wide-windowed studio
full of high cliffs. The sun tumbled down.

Since incest had thrown me from my parents' house
five years before, I hadn't had a real home,
but had travelled from friend to friend, job to short job,
without finding someplace I needed to go
or someone to live with—somewhere I could learn.

Red cliff-bodies stretched from the glistening surge
of a half-moon of beach as I made up the bed
and Brigid raced down to the water. I breathed,
feeling I was at home, in the place of a friend.

Act 1

Scene 1.

*The little house, by the shore of a large ocean. The winding road leads to the
house past large, dark, rounded cliffs. EVE is sitting on the porch in one of two
green wicker rockers, her bare feet up on a the railing, drawing spiral patterns
on a large pad of paper. Around her against the porch railings are propped large
stained glass panels made of beach-glass. Piles of beach-glass (larger than life)
are arranged by color on the floor around her.*

LILY (*approaching the porch*):
Good morning!

EVE:
Good morning—hello! You look tired.

LILY:
I've been walking all day.

EVE:
Would you like to come in?

LILY:
Thank you! I'm Lily.

EVE:
And my name is Eve.

LILY settles into one of the rockers and picks up the pad as EVE goes to get tea.

LILY:

One spiral shell wound in layers like sand,
one pebble left on the shore where it lands;
please lend me your voices, and some of your stories . . .
(*looking more intently at the paper*)
Spirals—bird wings—

EVE (*settling down with the tea*):
So tell me, Lily,
Where have you come from?

LILY (*simultaneously*):
Tell me, Eve,
Why have you stayed here?

They laugh and talk a little more slowly.

EVE:
So tell me, Lily,
Where have you come from?
Why have you come here?

LILY:
I hope to find safety with people again.
Tell me, Eve,
Why have you stayed here?

EVE:
My long-ago story still colors my days.

LILY *gets up and begins to walk restlessly about the house. She stops in front
of one of the piles of sea-glass and half-idly picks up one piece after another as*
EVE *walks over to her.*

LILY:
I hope to find safety with people again.
Incest threw me from my parents' house

26

five years ago. I haven't had a real home,
but have travelled from friend to friend, job to short job,
without finding someplace I needed to go

EVE:
My long-ago story still colors my days.

LILY:
Or someone to live with, somewhere I could learn . . .

They sit down together on the porch again and pick up their cups of tea.

EVE:
My long-ago story still colors my days.
Years ago, I was led from my home
and my minister husband. I was searching for strengths
fit for a woman, for dark, for the earth.

LILY:
I know what you mean, Eve! I need those things too!
But look what you've made here. Look how it glows.

EVE:
Yes, patterns of stained glass keep dreaming for me
around the white walls. The sad days are gone.
I have lived here for decades, in these small white rooms,
awakened by the shore.

LILY:
It's beautiful here. It could feel like a home.

EVE:
I've needed a friend. I know I'm getting old.
I should have a companion. Lily, please stay.
You can rent out the spare room.

LILY (*half to herself, half to* EVE, *as* EVE *sips at her tea and gazes at the ocean*):

I see your eyes leap like quick fish, I feel fire.
You laugh with me easily, you brace your foot
on the wide, sturdy railing.
Your two hands vibrate with so many lines
they are conscious with age. They rest free of each other . . .

KOURETES (*begins chanting*):
Isis, Astarte, Diana, Hecate, Demeter, Kali—Inanna

*LILY and EVE move over again to the piles of sea-glass. EVE begins to pick up
certain pieces and show them to LILY, introducing her to their shapes and colors.*

EVE:
Lily, please stay.
You can rent out the room
where the red dreaming cliffs
cup the half-moon of shore . . .

LILY:
No-one has heard me like you yet; I'll stay.
I'll rent the spare room.

They hug each other in delight.

Eve was a garden, and her words reached down
into the fertile, unashamed soil
to soak up the rain of a living, long story.
Her hair tossed white patterns bare trees could have made
in long winter sunlights, she was so old—
and as each quick season passed over her body
she had learned not to fill it with anyone's power
except her desire—to open it freely
and let the clear goddesses make it their own.

Years before, she had been led from her home
and her minister husband, searching for strengths
fit for a woman, for dark, for the earth.

28

Now patterns of stained glass kept dreaming for her
around the white walls. The sad days were gone.
Looking for sea-glass to place in her windows,
she led me to where smooth rocks puckered in
at the edge of the bay, and around the next curve.
"There," she'd say, "Look, Marie," "Open your eyes!"

Amber or lapis; thin dust on ice; moss;
iron; aching scentless lavender—
she fused together their old new shapes
with soft strips of lead in her studio room:
sistrum, spirals, gates, loaves, and eyebrows,
bellies, mountains, crescents and eyes,
all stained by sun, and scrubbed by salt—
And my pained days fell cool where the tumbling tamed;
fingers of earth's anxious ocean redeemed.

SCENE 2.

Silhouette of LILY *making a bed inside the house, unpacking.* EVE *is at her work table, assembling many small pieces of sea-glass into a complex, quilt-like pattern which she will Eventually solder together. She sings as she works.*

KOURETES (*chanting*):
    Isis, Astarte, Diana, Hecate, Demeter, Kali—Inanna

EVE:
    I am a garden and my words reach down
    into the fertile, unashamed soil
    to soak up the rain of a long, living story.
    My hair tosses patterns bare trees could have made
    in long winter sunlights, I am so old,
    and as each quick season passes over my body
    I have learned not to fill it with anyone's power
    except my desire—to open it freely
    and let the clear goddesses make it my own.

29

KOURETES:
  Isis, Astarte . . .

EVE:
  I hear the names of the goddesses . . .

  EVE *rises slowly.* ISIS *and* ASTARTE *emerge on stage and dance;* EVE
  sways with them, watching.

EVE:
  Isis, child of healing, heal me!
  Astarte, power of beginnings!

KOURETES:
  Isis, Astarte, Diana

EVE:
  Diana, clarity of moonlight, fill me!

  DIANA *and* HECATE *appear and join the other goddesses.*

EVE:
  Hecate, goddess of the crossroads, I will choose!

KOURETES:
  Isis, Astarte, Diana, Hecate, Demeter

  DEMETER *appears and joins the others.*

EVE:
  Demeter! Friend, earth-goddess, deep mother!

KOURETES:
  Isis, Astarte, Diana, Hecate, Demeter, Kali—

EVE:

Kali, death-dealer, balancer—

KOURETES:
   Isis, Astarte, Diana, Hecate, Demeter, Kali—
   Isis, Astarte, Diana, Hecate, Demeter, Kali—Inanna

KALI *and* INANNA *appear and join the others.*

EVE:
   Inanna!

A scream from Lily's room. LILY *comes running in. The goddesses vanish.*

LILY:
   Eve!

EVE (*hugging her*):
   What happened, Lily?!

LILY:
   I was afraid—something happened—I don't know—I was scared—I got a
   chill—I felt such fear—all of a sudden—

EVE:
   Lily. Let's go take a walk on the beach, ok?

Several years later, thinking she slept,
I stood by the ocean and saw morning clouds
rolling in on a wave like a memory of childhood.
That morning when Brigid and I climbed the cliff,
Eve was gone. And she had left me the house,
the stained glass that stretched and waited for light,
more gifts than I'd dreamed of.

SCENE 3.

EVE *and* LILY *walk down to the beach together. The house is visible above the beach, at the top of a flight of steep faded wooden stairs.*

They walk.

EVE:
Look! Here is a sea-glass to put in the windows—
Look, Lily, there!! Open your eyes!
Amber or lapis; thin dust on ice; moss;
iron; aching scentless lavender—

I'll fuse together their old new shapes
with soft strips of lead in my studio room—

LILY AND EVE:
sistrum, spirals, gates, loaves, and eyebrows,
bellies and mountains, crescents and eyes,
all stained by sun and scrubbed by salt.

LILY:
And my pained days fall cool where the tumbling is tamed,
fingers of anxious new ocean redeemed.

SCENE 4.

Eve's bedroom. EVE *is lying on a bed in the background.* LILY *is bending over the bed. Green light pours over the stage.*

LILY (*to Eve*):
Your face is so peaceful. But your eyes say goodbye.

EVE:
Yes, I am peaceful.
I know I am leaving my house with you, dear.
I'll leave you the ocean I love, and the sound

of waves filled with goddesses, mountains that move

LILY:
   Is there anything else, Eve? Anything else
   that you need to say to me?

EVE:
   Go find Demeter, when I am gone.
   She will remind you of earth's deepest heart.

KOURETES:
   Gates and spirals, loaves, nipples, waves,
   bellies, mountains, crescents and eyes . . .

EVE:
   Always remember the strangeness of love.
   Both death and life, are the goddesses' heart.
   Goodbye, dear Lily,

LILY:
   Goodbye, dear Eve.

EVE:
   Goodbye, my Lily! The goddesses are here.

LILY (*tiptoes to front of stage*):
   her eyes said goodbye
   from those depths as if I were the lost one,
   the one who traveled. All she had done
   served to hold the centuries, linked through her bones,
   so they showered out onto me as I watch her—

EVE *begins to toss. The light turns from green to pink.* LILY *runs to the bed.*

LILY:
   Eve!!!!!!!!!!!!!!!!!!!!!!
   (*rising*)

33

If I listen still for her footsteps,
only the tides hear, and wash them aside;
only the tides give them a beginning.

KOURETES:
Gates and spirals, loaves, nipples, waves,
bellies, mountains, crescents and eyes . . .
Only the tides give them a beginning.

There is no end if there was no beginning.

LILY *leaves the room blindly, heading for the beach.*

Her face was so peaceful,
kept in the smooth touching patches of colors.
Pink and green light from the east windows

covered her skin, and her eyes said goodbye
from those depths as if I were the lost one,
the one who travelled. All she had done
served to hold the centuries linked through her bones
so they showered out onto us as we watched her.
If I listen still for her footsteps,
only the tides hear, and wash them aside;
only the tides give them a beginning.
only the tides hear, and wash them aside.

There is no end if there was no beginning.

SCENE 5.

The beach and the stairs outside the house. Strong-colored lights change in the sky.

LILY:
I am hunting for Eve in the tickling water
that crashes at edges endlessly. I startle . . .

She screams suddenly at the sight of a sudden low cloud, very dark with extremely bright edges.

KOURETES:
Taken by fullness, low reaching cloud,
thickened in shadow

Fighting an impulse to cover her head and run, LILY walks back towards the steps.

LILY:
Peach-gold with richness, inscribed down to light,
filled through all my dreaming. I darken awake.

Silently, awed, she climbs the steps. The sun is low in the sky. On the stairs near the top is sitting a small child with black hair and a headdress: the great goddess ISIS.

LILY gasps and walks slowly up the last steps to Isis, who is crying.

KOURETES:
Isis!!! Isis!!! Isis!!!!!

Isis, Astarte, Diana....

Isis! Isis! Isis!!!

LILY:
Isis! Isis! You're crying, . . .
staring right at me . . .
right on the steps of my house . . .

ISIS *sobs.*

LILY (*touching her*):

(You're real.) This is stranger
than Eve's death, but not much.

ISIS *keeps crying.*

LILY:
You're just a child. Here, come to the house.

Isis' bracelets and anklets jangle as LILY *takes her shoulder and leads her towards the door.*

LILY:
Here, watch the step. That's right. Come on in.

ISIS *is still crying slightly as they go into the house through the already-open back door.*

Book 2: Isis

That long remembered, remembering day
with Brigid, whose thick tail was dripping
like a torn flag mourning down the gray shore,
I hunted for Eve in that tickling water
that crashed at the edges endlessly. . . . I startle,
taken by fullness, to find a low cloud,
thickened like shadow and cold as with age,
peach-gold with richness inscribed down to light,
fill through all my dreaming. I darken awake.

Then in the quiet, I walked up the cliff,
pensively, following Brigid, who saw her,
and stopped still, which is strange. She usually
bounded up to strangers. This was a small child,
perched on the third step, her head hardly reaching
over the sixth step. Her hands lay like stones
heavily resting on parallel kneecaps.
At last I noticed what should have been strangest:
her black hair, thick and oily, framing

a looming headdress made of a mirror,
columned by tree trunks and snakes. She was crying,
almost formally, staring straight at us,
right on the steps of my house. This was stranger
than Eve's death, but not much; I touched her.
Then, shaking my stupor, I guided her shoulder
in through the back door, left open that morning.
Hesitant at first, then deliberate,
picking her way through the raincoats and boots,

her arms clicking occasionally with bracelets,
she padded on her bare feet. She must have been ten.
Shadowed always by Eve, I was grateful to see her. . . .
I stop and remember the last faded morning,

when her slow hand wandered back from her hair
and fingered the pillow . . . as if she were trying
to hold the patterns of the currents of form
that depths enter, flow through, and leave as we come.

SCENE 6.

The kitchen and living room of the house.

Enter LILY *and* ISIS.

LILY:
Here. Sit down.

She pushes ISIS *down on the sofa but* ISIS *gets up immediately and follows her into the kitchen.*

LILY (*turns on the flame under the kettle and turns around*):
I see.
You don't want to be alone?
Hold this. Here.

She hands ISIS *a tray.*

LILY:
OK. Gingersnaps. *She gets down the box.* That seems just right for you, Isis. Do you like these?

ISIS *eats one and likes it.*

LILY:
I thought so. Let's see. *She rummages among jars of loose tea.* Black tea . . . you're too young . . . Chamomile . . . peppermint . . . Jasmine. That's it. Jasmine. Rich, like you. Strong, like you. Isis.

KOURETES:
Isis. Isis.

ISIS *is standing with great dignity still holding the tray.* LILY *pours the tea as she stands there. They go to the sofa and sit down.*

ISIS:
Immmmmmmmmmmmmmmmmmm

LILY *looks up.*

ISIS (*putting down her gingersnap*):
Immmmmmmmmm Wooooooooooooooooooooooooooooooo

LILY *watches.*

Isis:
Immmmmmmmmm Wooooooooooooooooooooooooooooooo Uhhhhhh

ISIS *stands up suddenly. She stands in front of the sofa with her arms crossed tightly on her chest.*

LILY *gets up.*

They walk together to the window and stare out at the setting sun and the beach.

ISIS (*chants again*):
ImmmmmmmmmmmWOOOOOOOOOOOOOOOOOOUh

LILY *joins her.*

Still seeing beach pebbles until my eyes wavered

back towards the water, I smiled at the child
and made jasmine tea. I thought she looked scared. . . .
Now in the kitchen, without Eve to help me,
I am alone, my own life before me,

and a thin voice is chanting. . . . It seemed to reach me,
to make more sense. I pulled more gingersnaps
out of the box. Then I went to the table
and set them down while she stood there, swaying
in front of the couch. She seemed bigger, inside,

shorter than I of course, but more vivid, more urgent.
After a moment, we sat down together
in the sunset-red vortex of late afternoon.
Her brown toes gripping at the thin green carpet
transformed me and transfixed my senses.

The sun goes below the horizon during the following scene.

LILY (*coming to the front of the stage, leaving Isis by the window*):
Eve! I hear her
and something stops me and moves me away—
as if I came questioning like huge water—

KOURETES:
Gates and spirals, loaves, nipples, waves,
bellies, mountains, crescents and eyes . . .
Only the tides give them a beginning.

ISIS:
ImmmmmmmmmmWOOOOOOOOOOOOOOOOOUh

LILY:
What is she saying? What is she saying?

As Isis stands at the window, LILY *goes outside and bends down to the earth
as if listening to its heart.*

LILY:
What is she saying? What is she saying?

KOURETES:
>   Gates and spirals, loaves, nipples, waves,
>   bellies, mountains, crescents and eyes . . .

ISIS:
>   "Please take me out to gather my brother"

LILY:
>   as if I came questioning like huge water—
>   and something stops me and moves me away—

ISIS AND KOURETES:
>   "Please take me out to gather my brother"

LILY:
>   and something—

ISIS AND KOURETES:
>   "Please take me out to gather"

LILY:
>   Please take me

ISIS AND KOURETES:
>   "Please take me out to gather my brother"

ISIS, KOURETES, AND LILY:
>   "Please take me out to gather my brother
>   up through the stars that have poured out like milk
>   over my losses, and I'll join the night sky."

LILY:
>   These are the languages I finally know
>   for dark-eyed, moon-caped Isis.

ISIS, KOURETES, AND LILY:
>   "Please take me out to gather my brother

up through the stars that have poured out like milk
over my losses, and I'll join the night sky."

LILY:

How could I say I'll help her?
It echoes in languages I finally know
for dark-eyed, moon-caped Isis.
I'll help her.
I'll help her; I know I need to let her go.
I know there will still be another
goddess for me.

KOURETES:

as if I came questioning from the huge water—

LILY:

She reached out her hand and I told her goodbye.
Then in the light falling below the thin moon,
I watched that small body vanish and grow.

KOURETES:

I watched that small body vanish and grow.

Changed light skidded around the walls.
She sipped tea with both hands and then stood up,
suddenly, in a changeless position,
arms crossed tightly on her chest, and stared down

out at the beach. And then I heard her . . .
and something stops me and moves me away—
back to the beach with the answering curves—
as if I came questioning from the huge water—
for the first time, she spoke clearly, saying—
"Please take me out to gather my brother"
—as if I came questioning from the huge water—
—and something stops me and moves me away—
"up through the stars that have poured out like milk

over my losses, and I'll join the night sky."

Then calm emptiness
filled the room.

Scene 7.

The sun has set; it is now dark. Lily *and* Isis *walk down the stairs to the beach under many stars, including Isis' brother the constellation Orion, as the* Kouretes *sing.*

Kouretes:
Orion—Osiris—weaves his sword-light
through the half-open, half-alive sky.

Lily *and* Isis *stand on the beach.*

Isis:
Now the ocean is full and trembling,
and the shore is trembling and full,

Kouretes:
Orion—Osiris—weaves his sword-light
through the half-open, half-alive sky.

Lily:
Reach out your hand and I'll tell you goodbye.
Then go on the tender keeper of water,
tender keeper of land into water

Isis *reaches out her hand.*

How did I say I'd help her?
It echoed in languages I finally knew
for dark-eyed, moon-caped Isis. I helped her,
knowing there would still be another

goddess for me. Late in the dream,
as Orion—Osiris—wove his sword-light
down through the half-open, half-alive sky,
Brigid and I carried her down the cliff,

and I set her down.

LILY:
    Goodbye, Isis.

ISIS *walks away and is swallowed in darkness under the stars.*

KOURETES:
    Now the ocean is full and trembling,
    and the shore is trembling and full,
    In the light that falls below the thin moon,
    Orion—Osiris—weaves his sword-light
    and Isis is with him, Isis is with him,
    wet with drinking the pouring of starlight,
    Isis is with him, Isis is with him.

    The stars suddenly shine brighter and more numerous.
    A stylized figure of ISIS, *mask or puppet, comes out of the darkness and accompanies* LILY *up the steps. It will be with her from now on.*

and I set her down. She had asked to be carried
to the shore, which was trembling and full,
and when her feet sank, like mine and like Brigid's,
deep into the beach where night was believing
in the sand-borne fountains of millions of stars—
in that tender keeper of land into water—
she reached out her hand and we told her good bye.
Then in the light falling below the thin moon,
we watched that small body vanish, and grow.

    LILY *slowly climbs the steps once more,* "ISIS" *behind her. At the top of the steps is the altar or stone of* ASTARTE.

44

LILY *stops in her tracks. The stone glows.* "ISIS" *runs madly around the stone.*

LILY *circles the stone warily.*

LILY (*getting her bearings*):
It was the stone, solid, rounded,
dense, warmed from within by a universe,
over three feet of carved gold sandstone,
right in the path. I knew I had found her,
The other goddess Isis said would come,

ISIS AND LILY:
balanced on the brim between water and land,
full of the great guest and lost for a time
in the new night that is darker than the old,
with sacred Astarte, a goddess of earth—

KOURETES:
Isis, Astarte, Diana, Hecate, Demeter, Kali, Inanna

LILY *moves the stone away from the edge of the cliff. Rain is starting to fall in a strong shower.* LILY *goes into the house and lies down to sleep while the rain pours on the stone.*

All goddesses dance as LILY *sleeps.*

KOURETES:
Isis, Astarte, Diana, Hecate, Demeter, Kali—Inanna

End of Act I.

Act II

Scene 1.

Outside the cottage. The rain is gradually stopping. The Kouretes *are chanting repeatedly: "Isis, Astarte, Diana, Hecate, Demeter, Kali—Inanna."*

The stone, on a green stage. Many small saplings appear around the stone in a sporadic rhythm.

Lily *wakes and comes out of the house.*

Lily:
> Morning is easy, after a night
> of goddess-rain and the love of Astarte.
> Morning is easy; fog is open.
> Morning is easy, morning is easy.
> Morning is easy, rain has brought me
> to the morning Astarte promised.
> Morning is easy, morning is easy—
> the trees! The trees! Trees are born!

Kouretes:
> All night, roots forced their way through darkness.

Lily (*coming closer to look at the trees*):
> They speak like aspens, though stronger than aspens . . .

Book 3: Astarte

Wet with the pouring drinking of starlight,
I stumbled, shocked, up the path to my own house,
where I was suddenly forced to be calm
by the new presence of what she had promised.
It was the stone, solid, rounded,
dense, warmed from within by a universe,
over three feet of carved gold sandstone,
right in the path. I knew I had found her,
balanced on the brim between water and land.

Under the dog-star that shone much brighter
with the sparkle of the dried tears of a child
down on my hair, I was empty, excited,
full of the great guest and lost for a time,
in the new night that was darker than the old.
I half-rolled, half-rocked her to safety
in front of the house, settled her by the stairs—
sacred Astarte, a goddess of earth—
went in, lay down, and then the rain poured.

Brigid lay at my feet and whimpered.
All night, roots forced their way through darkness.
Morning was easy. I was born.
trees had sprouted around the stone.
They spoke like aspens, though stronger than aspens . . .

KOURETES:
    They spoke like aspens, though stronger than aspens . . .

VOICE OF ASTARTE:
    Then plant me now

KOURETES:
    Astarte is calling,

VOICE OF ASTARTE:
　　Then plant me now

KOURETES:
　　from ancient wind-beaten pillars,

VOICE OF ASTARTE:
　　Then plant me now

KOURETES:
　　from deep-rooted altars all over the planet,

VOICE OF ASTARTE:
　　Then plant me now
　　Then plant me now

KOURETES:
　　Then plant me now

During the chanting, LILY *goes to get a shovel and bucket and bends to dig out the trees from the earth and pile them in the bucket.*

KOURETES:
　　"then plant me now," I heard Astarte
　　calling, from ancient wind-beaten pillars,
　　from deep-rooted altars all over the planet,
　　till I sang to myself, as I started to dig them,

　　for the vision of Isis, the memory of Eve,
　　and for myself, for the growth of Marie.

LILY (*putting the last tree in her bucket, straightening up*):
　　I will plant these trees for Astarte,
　　wherever they take me, wherever I go—
　　up and down the coast of Oregon,
　　up and down the coast of California,
　　on the gray beaches and next to the gray waves,

I will plant these trees for Astarte.
I'll look for the friend of Eve's in San Francisco.

She walks off the stage as the lights dim.

SCENE 2.

Morning. A road with a small town in the distance.

LILY *is walking along the road, wearing a backpack decorated with spirals and goddess-eyes, carrying the trees in a bucket.*

LILY:
> The rusty leaves of Astarte's trees,
> the star-studded green leaves keep guiding me on,
> to move through my life to the next place of worship . . .

She stops to plant one of the trees and walks again.

LILY:
> Night after night and day after day,
> carrying the trees to plant for Astarte,
> day after day and night after night,

She passes through a dark glade or tunnel and reemerges.

LILY:
> Night after night and day after day

LILY *enters a town and walks into a churchyard with old graves, where she puts her sleeping bag on the ground next to the church wall.*

LILY:
> It looks dark here; the moonlight is blocked by walls.

She shivers and looks around, puts her backpack carefully on the ground, and lies down in the sleeping bag.

SCENE 3.

Night. Moon over the grassy lawn in the shade of the looming, shadowy church as LILY *sleeps.*

KOURETES:
by the wall of a church in a small dark town

LILY (*startling awake, murmuring*):
What's happening?!

She settles back uneasily to sleep. A few minutes pass.

The shadow of a man appears clearly on the church wall in the moonlight.

KOURETES:
by the wall of a church in a small dark town

LILY *moves in her sleep.*

MAN (*crouching over her, whispering*):
Who's here?—
Who's this?—
A woman! A woman!
Listen—breathing!
(*louder whisper*)
Thy will be done!
(*He goes to her backpack.* LILY *stirs again.*)
What does she have here?
Books! Books! A candle!
Bells! Books of the devil!
Clothes! More clothes!
More books of the devil!

LILY (*waking and whispering to herself in fear*):
A shadow! A shadow!

MAN:
Oh, devil's work, she-devil, evil one . . .

LILY:
Stop that! What are you doing to my things!

MAN:
Evil symbols, witches' symbols!

LILY:
The symbols in memory of Eve . . .

Brigid rooted in the earth to free them.
I brought a bucket and filled it until
"Sing to me, now," all her trees whispered to me,
with cool leaves rattling sharper than stones
that hems of cold water have poured on the beaches.
And the next day I started moving through Oregon
to plant those altars for Astarte,

to look for a friend of Eve's in San Francisco,
to move through my life to the next place of worship,
with only Brigid, my backpack, the trees—
thinking and walking, sleeping outside,
planting, hitchhiking, moving southward.
I rooted my altars, chanting and comforted,
and the first nights went quietly, with no clue
of the thing that would happen. Letting the rusty,
star-studded green leaves keep guiding me on,

waving above the earth where I left them,
I travelled till the eighth night.

MAN (*menacing, holding her things*):
  She-demon, get out!
  Get out of here!

  LILY (*pulling herself out of the sleeping bag*):
  Stop, you maniac! Stop!

MAN (*grabbing her*):
  Witch! Witch!
  Abomination in a place of God!

KOURETES (*still chanting*):
  by the wall of a church—
  by the wall of a church—

MAN:
  Filthy she-devil!

LILY:
  Let go of my body! Sacred to the Goddess!

MAN (*throwing her down on the ground*):
  Sacrilege! Pagan! Witch! I'll show you!

LILY:
  Leave me alone! I'll get out of your churchyard!
  Let me go!

MAN:
  Let you go now!?
  Abomination, filthy witch!

LILY:
  Stop! Stop!

MAN:

Let you go? Now say who is God!

LILY (*shrieking*):
    Stop!!!!!

MAN:
    Say it! Say it! Say who is God!
    Evil she-devil! Witch! You say it!

LILY (*making a mighty effort*):
    For the Goddess, for Isis the child, for Eve!
    Insane vicious man! Coward! I crush you!
    With the power of the Goddess I crush your hand!

*She tears one hand free and pulls with all her strength on one of his fingers,
spraining it. He shrieks in pain and pulls his hand back.*

MAN:
    Witch! Filthy demon! How dare you!
    You defiled this place! Abomination!
    Filth! She-devil! Pagan! Evil!

LILY *pushes free, grabs most of her things and stuffs them into the backpack,
and runs.*
Darkness.

That night we'd settled in
by the wall of a church in a small dark town.
Brigid was barking when I opened my eyes.
It looked dark. Moonlight was blocked by walls.
I saw a shadow, then: a righteous man
thick in the half-light from the street-lights,
rummaging furiously in my backpack,
throwing books and tools on the ground,

cursing the symbols I'd just painted there:
(pentacle, mirror of Isis, waves

in memory of Eve at sea). "You witch!"
he shouted, and grabbed me. His hands dripped with sweat.
"What are you doing in this place of God!!"
The next thing I knew, screaming he'd teach me,
kicking at Brigid, he had torn my light skirt
and was raping me, furious, forcing me down.
Finally I pulled back so hard on a finger

that he had braced on the ground, I broke it;
while he bellowed and froze in pain, I struggled
free, and grabbed most of my things. We ran,
four legs and two, like wind off that mountain,
barking and crying at the hatred behind us,
strong with the fury of Astarte around us.

LILY:

> Days and days with the ocean near me,
> filling up my ears and my body,

Trembling, we ran into a quiet graveyard
where all day, under a dripping rain-tarp,
we watched spiders beading the light with strong weaving.

Two trees were left of the nine that had grown
out on the cliff. Still numb with grief and anger,
I planted one in that town the next morning.
Three children watched and helped with the chanting.
Through their easy faces, I felt wisdom come.
Each tree was strong. Before I went home,
I knew that I wanted to plant the last tree
far down the coast, in San Francisco,
the place I had come from before I found Eve.

SCENE 4.

LILY *is walking, with* ISIS *and* ASTARTE *following her. She has one tree left in her bucket.*

LILY:
Days and days with the ocean near me,
filling up my ears and my body,
with my feet padding, padding,
over the roads and beaches and highways,
through more towns, cities, suburbs and malls,

KOURETES:
granite, basalt, quartz and sandstone,

The skyline of San Francisco is visible in the distance.

LILY:
Metal and sunshine!
Metal and sunshine!
Look through the power lines,
look at the hills!
The air drenches a coastal city!
A goddess can grow her own light to move in!
(*She approaches the city, down a hill.*)
The air drenches this coastal city;
a goddess slips past the sun-hard buildings.
She startles, because she grows her own light
to move in.

DIANA, *in the distance, moves just after* LILY *describes her movements, as if her movement is evoked by Lily's words.* DIANA *enters a doorway marked "Artemis Cafe."*

LILY (*starting to move on*):
There is Diana! I know it is she!
Diana is a maze as I see her
glide through a city embedded with mica,
(LILY *walks downhill.*)
onto that doorstep of bright blue cement.

55

Diana's maze is a forest of pillars.
Diana's maze is the maze of the doorway.
Amaze me Diana, amaze me, Diana . . .

Sudden darkness on the stage. HECATE (*very tall, stooped, eccentric, wearing a rust-black cloak*) *appears right in front of* LILY, *humming.*

LILY (*panicked*):
Who are you? What are you?

HECATE:
Hecate, goddess of the crossroads.

KOURETES:
Crossroads, crossroads

HECATE:
Hecate! Queen of the witches.

LILY:
Hecate, goddess of the crossroads.

HECATE:
Hecate! Queen of the witches.

LILY:
What are you telling me? What are you telling me?

HECATE *points to Lily's stomach.* LILY *gasps and clutches herself. Darkness.*

When the lights go back up, HECATE *has disappeared.* LILY *runs furiously, still holding the tree and her backpack, circling back to the door of the cafe.*

BOOK 4: DIANA

Days and days with the ocean near me,
filling up my ears and my body,
with my dog's feet padding, padding,
over the roads and beaches and highways,
granite, basalt, quartz and sandstone,
walking, hitchhiking, walking, hitchhiking,
through more towns, cities, suburbs and malls,
we came to the city, metal and sunshine,
gneiss, hornblende, mica and feldspar.

Looking through power lines, we walked downhill
into a street in the Mission district.
Metal branches held lights, signs, Diana.
She crossed towards a dark blue doorway with stars
scattered around it. Brigid was barking
with excitement, her thick wolf's tail
circled above her in a coiling of delight.
In the air that drenches a coastal city,
a goddess, slipping past sun-hard buildings,

startles, because she grows her own light
to move in. It was amazing to see her
glide on that sidewalk embedded with mica,
past a doorstep of bright blue cement,
and make her way through a forest of pillars
into the doorway. We started to follow,
Brigid wild with the need to find her.
I stopped and bent down to calm her barking
when a tall, stooped, eccentric woman,

wearing a rusty cloak and a frown,
pushed through the crowd that was moving around us,
grabbed Brigid's collar, and pulled her away,
the cape flapping next to her like bat wings
vanishing around a distant building.

I hesitated a second, shocked,
and then started running around the corner
where they had gone, weaving through people's stares,
still carrying the tree, and my backpack.

Panting, two streets later, I gave up,
losing the small sight of cape and dark fur.
I found a phone and called the police,
then stood there trembling with memory and anger,
trying to understand why this woman—
of whom I had registered only her eyes,
very sharp and so dark they looked vacant,
but utterly focused, although they were hollow—
would have taken my single companion,

and how a death, a rape, and a pregnancy
could have left room for the loss of my Brigid.
Finally, shaking and furious with tears,
still exhausted, I felt my solitude
and saw the steep slope that led in sunlight
to the blue doorway. I remembered Diana,
how Eve had told me I had to meet her,
and I walked down the hill, and over the threshold.
It was darker inside than I'd wanted,

but soon I saw it was a cafe
with deep blue walls decorated with moons,
just the way Eve had described it to me.

SCENE 6.

LILY *walks into the small café, which has deep blue walls decorated with moons, and contains five or six tables. All the tables are empty except for* DI-ANA *sitting in the far corner and the three* KOURETES, *one a waiter, sitting alone at other tables.* LILY *sits down with her head on her hands.*

LILY:

Hecates, Hecate . . .

(*pauses*)

Hecate, Hecate, what have you told me?

First a death, then a rape, now a pregnancy?

Hecate, Hecate, now am I pregnant?

The waiter rises and comes to Lily's table.

LILY:

A bowl of soup, please. Some bread.

(*waiter leaves*)

Queen of the Witches,

of whom I registered only her eyes,

very sharp and so dark they looked vacant,

but utterly focused, although they were hollow—

Hecate—Hecate, did you want something?

Still you said nothing, spinning and thrumming.

I looked up to see you and found you were gone.

(*Waiter returns with food*)

(*Still to herself*):

Hecate, Hecate, what have you told me?

First a death, then a rape, now a pregnancy?

Hecate, Hecate, now am I pregnant?

Hecate, goddess of the crossroads

looming above me, your face like a tomb,

as you enveloped my day with your darkness,

the oldest, haggard face of the moon

swung into place like a sky above me,

covering me with a solitude.

WAITER:

There is Diana. She wants to talk to you.

LILY *turns to see* DIANA *waving at her from her chair.*

I found my breath, ordered soup and some bread,
rested a while, and watched Diana,
who sat two tables away. Then I said, "I'm Marie.
I'm a friend of Eve's." Her glittering glance
flashed and paused. She laid pale hands open
flat on her table. "Hi! Let's go outside,"

and she grabbed her narrow satchel and paid.
High out in Dolores Park, we sat quietly
after the climb and shared water from my backpack.
She remembered Eve well, and was very anxious
to hear of her last days; smiled at Isis and Astarte;
and she shook at the rape, as the pastel skyline
flecked over with shadows. When I told her
about the loss of Brigid, she sighed.
"That was Hecate. I know her well."

"She's so strange. Is she crazy?" I asked her.
Diana laughed. "Crazy? No more than I am . . .
Where are you going next? Back to Oregon?
Give me the address. I'll make her call you."

LILY (*gets up and walks over to Diana's table*):
    Hi, I'm Lily. I'm a friend of Eve's.
    Eve told me that I might find you here.

They sit together talking quietly as the waiter brings Lily's food and she eats.

LILY AND DIANA:
    Hecate, goddess of the crossroads
    looming above us, your face like a tomb,
    as you enveloped the day with your darkness,
    the oldest, haggard face of the moon
    swung into place like a sky above us,
    covered us with your old solitude.

DIANA *rises suddenly.*

60

DIANA:
Lily, the moon's up now. Let's go outside!

SCENE 7.

Outside. Dusk. A crescent moon, with the sound of the ocean nearby. LILY
and DIANA *plant the last tree from Lily's bucket together, in a circle of three
flat stones near a forest, dance together in a simple circle.*

Near the high coast, in the Presidio,
we planted a tree within three flat stones.
I welcomed the wake of the moon reflected
through Diana, the darting-eyed woman,
her slow feet keeping time with the ocean.

LILY (*stopping to look at the moon*):
The trees are all planted. It's time to move on.

DIANA:
What will you do now? Where will you go?

LILY:
Eve has a friend in Ohio, a gardener;
Eve and Demeter once lived there together.
Eve told me she is wise, and she loved her.
Yes, it's time for moving. I need to move on.

They hug goodbye.

End of Act II.

Book 5: Hecate

When I finally got home, the house seemed emptier
Without Brigid. Waves crawled more silently
onto the beach, with no-one to chase them.
Winter was coming, and each night the moon
grew bigger and thicker, and each day the sky
was grayer. I gave up on Brigid.
I had thought I would settle back to my old life,
sculpt in peace, and walk by the sea;
Where was my home, if not by the ocean?

Was there another place for me?
But it was all different without my companion,
and something seemed to say I should go.
So, after a month, I decided to change,
to gather myself and move on, when I'd rested.
Dreaming in a daze, I was packing,
when, one morning, as I boxed some china,
musing and only half-knowing I planned,
a guttural, strange voice called out, "Marie!"

Who was it? Hecate, coming this early
out of that dawn light to knock on my door?
Leaving puddles of sunlight to deepen,
kicking boxes out of the way,
I ran to the front room. I knew she'd appear
just as I opened my old weathered door,
in a dark coat, with her eyes hooded closely
by skin like old roots, but gleaming with a flame
that echoes its ashes. She reached out to touch me

as soon as she saw me, one hand on my wrist,
and in the cool hush, I led her inside
to sit on the couch, in the same spot where Eve
had sat with me night after night in the dusk.
Her presence, a shadow, stopped my house around her,

darkening a spot in the cool sunny room.
There, in the fallen starkness of moving,
where no objects were haloed or solid,
I had nothing to say. I couldn't be angry.

Silently, soon after she had sat down
and refused to drink anything, she got Brigid in
from her old black car. Ecstatically barking
amid my relief and Hecate's triumph
at having kept her away for so long,
she soon settled down as if nothing had changed.
"It looks like you're moving—-where are you going?"
asked Hecate. I told her the choices I had,
meek at her voice and resigned to her power.

She seemed to grow taller while I was talking,
and when I had finished she started to hum,
intently, as if a huge top were spinning.
Hecate, goddess of the crossroads
looming above me, your face like a tomb,
as you enveloped my day with your darkness,
the oldest, haggard face of the moon
swung into place like a sky above me,
covering me with a solitude.

Hecate—Hecate, did you want something?
I offered you food and drink and a view,
but you sat there, closed and unmoving
as if you had something important to say,
though still you said nothing, spinning and thrumming.
I looked up to see you and found you were gone.
When she had gone, I walked down to the shore
to say goodbye to the rocks and the bay.
In a huge ancient boulder, washed by the sea,

which I had never examined before,
I saw lines that spoke like a face in the moon

and I knew I was going to travel to Ohio.
Eve had a friend there, a gardener; she'd told me
often of how they had lived there together,
and reminded me I could always go there
for guidance. I needed someone now,
now I was pregnant, and empty, and hollow.
It was time for moving. I needed to go.

So, with everything finished and sealed,
my boxes in storage with friends, some mementoes,
including Eve's thimble and all of her glass,
the day the new owners were coming, I said
a kind of goodbye to the memory of Eve,
goodbye to the stone and the trees by the door,
the gray morning ocean, the hills by the bay,
and started, just Brigid to tell me she'd been there,
leaving a hollow space in the morning.

Act III

Scene 1.

Demeter's garden in Ohio: tall ripening tomatoes mixed with many herbs and flowers, near the side of a large barn. DEMETER *is picking peas and dropping them into a large tin mixing bowl as* KOURETES *chant repeatedly, to the traditional tune:* "Isis, Astarte, Diana, Hecate, Demeter, Kali—Inanna."

LILY *approaches silently and watches as Demeter sings to herself.*

DEMETER:
> Long grass pushes up under the trees,
> hyssop, bee balm, lavender, chicory,
> mallow, johnny jump up, love in a mist,
> coneflower, blackeyed susan, broccoli,
> in my circular garden that curves from the earth. . .

64

LILY (*to herself and audience*):
　　Her hands are as wide, cool, and earth-stained
　　as mossy old rocks that a forest has patiently
　　grown up around, died around, fallen near.

DEMETER:
　　spine in the planet, blood in the wind,
　　as I drop the peas in the aluminum bowl. . .
　　spine in the planet, blood in the wind . . .

KOURETES (*under the following conversation*):
　　spine in the planet, blood in the wind . . .

LILY:
　　The arms of the planet are holding me alive.

DEMETER:
　　I know everything old about Eve

LILY:
　　Eve, the face of Demeter teaches me,

DEMETER:
　　rose from fire as well as earth:

LILY AND DEMETER (*standing to face each other*):
　　Eve was the full gleam of light on the water.

DEMETER:
　　Eve fell beside me, and rose and fell;
　　dark Eve, my own loss, my heartbeat, my sister,

LILY:
　　Eve speaks to me often without loss or damage
　　in my heart from the place of the dead,
　　the place of the openings that I have found.

LILY AND DEMETER:
Eve fell beside me, and rose and fell

LILY *crouches to help* DEMETER.

DEMETER (*murmuring quietly as she works*):
hyssop, bee balm, lavender, chicory,
mallow, johnny jump up, love in a mist,
coneflower, blackeyed susan, broccoli,
in my circular garden that curves from the earth. . .

Book 6: Demeter

As we stood on a curb in Ohio,
Brigid so glad to be with me again
after two days in the luggage compartment,
fresh sun shining into the bright spring,
so much denser, more humid than Oregon,
life seemed just starting. I phoned Demeter
for directions; I knew she'd be there,
since she had told me to phone from the bus stop
and that she'd be outside, working in the garden.

So Demeter found me, or rather, I found her
when her tomatoes were nodding and green
under the shelter of the side of her barn
near an acre of fields, wild with an orchard,
the long grass pushing up under the trees,
and hyssop, bee balm, lavender, chicory,
mallow, johnny jump up, love in a mist,
coneflower, blackeyed susan, lavender, broccoli,
in her circular garden that curved from the earth.

KOURETES:
>   Here is the mother who'd watched her own daughter
>   given away, and ruined the earth,
>   who now put out leaves, and nurtured the earth,

When we walked up, she was crouched in that circle,
picking peas from a strong tangled vine.
I waited and watched, while her mountainous body
filled my vision until I was quiet,
and the arms of the planet held me alive.
Her hands were as wide, cool, and earth-stained
as mossy old rocks that a forest has patiently
grown up around, died around, fallen near,
and pulls through the earth. Then my body was hers,

spine in the planet, blood in the wind,
as she dropped the peas in the aluminum bowl,
and sparks turned my thinking into its own waves.

DEMETER (*murmuring quietly in the background*):
    Caves run hollow until I can fill them
    with silent energies seeding new quiet . . .

    LILY *stands up suddenly at the word "crystals" and speaks as* DEMETER *continues murmuring.*

DEMETER:
    . . . crystals to form, and roots to come down
    into their veins; with water that pushes.
    with stems reaching, trunks reaching, leaves setting bone.

"Turn," I thought, and she turned around towards me,
smiling easily, just like Eve,
looking up at me while her face danced
in joyful images deep in its crevices.
I knew everything old about Eve then,
everything I had wanted to know,

while the planet shifted around me.
Eve, the face of Demeter now taught me,
rose from fire as well as earth:
Eve was the full gleam of light on the water.

LILY (*forcefully*):
    I'd been invaded; the baby was not mine.
    Why should I carry it?

Here with the mother who'd watched her own daughter
given away, and ruined the earth,
who now put out leaves, and nurtured the earth,
Eve fell beside me, and rose and fell;
dark Eve, my own loss, my heartbeat, my sister,

spoke to me often without loss or damage
in my heart from the place of the dead,
the place of the openings that I had found.

LILY (*forcefully*):
    I'd been invaded; the baby was not mine.
    Why should I carry it?

KOURETES:
    Coneflowers blew
    fuschia and silent, as if there was laughter,

LILY:
    from the breeze that was suddenly simpler,
    as if there could once more be joy. It has been
    months since I'd felt like myself, like Lily;
    months since my life has moved for me.

Idly, I'd been pulling deeply
at some weeds growing down in the herbs.
I made a small pile on the ground beside me.
I thought again about the decision, and suddenly
I felt very tired, and very afraid,

DEMETER (*finishing picking and rising, stretching*):
    When my darling Persephone was young,
    she cried every time I pulled weeds. It was hard
    to see that. It's hard to let go. We need to.

I felt very tired, and very afraid,
and, suddenly, filled with the earth's oldest memories,

held by Demeter in an echo of caves.
Caves run hollow until she can fill them
with silent energies seeding new quiet
crystals to form, and roots to come down

into their veins; with water that pushes.
with stems reaching, trunks reaching, leaves setting bone.
I'd been invaded; the baby was not mine.
Why should I carry it? Coneflowers blew
fuschia and silent, as if there was laughter,

DEMETER *puts her arm around* LILY. *They go inside the barn together.*

KOURETES:
    silent energies seeding new quiet
    crystals to form, and roots to come down
    into their veins; with water that pushes.
    with stems reaching, trunks reaching, leaves setting . . .

SCENE 2.

A rainy highway, with a small house in the distance. If possible the Serpent Mound, an ancient earthwork in the shape of a long snake, is visible. KOURETES *at the side of the stage.*

LILY *steps off a bus, lifts her coat up to cover her head, and begins to walk up the road.*

KOURETES:
    The other heart has begun its beating
    The other heart has begun its beating
    in the rich cave, the long silence

LILY (*as she walks*):
    The other heart has begun its beating
    in the rich cave, the long silence
    the hoping morning that was my womb.

KOURETES:
    The other heart has begun its beating
    The other heart has begun its beating

I'd been invaded; the baby was not mine.
Why should I carry it? Coneflowers blew
fuschia and silent, as if there was laughter,

LILY:

    Through my belly run knife-hard images
    to my body and to my heart.
    The hate that touched me on the mountain
    is still thriving, making a silence

Why should I carry it? Coneflowers blew
fuschia and silent, as if there was laughter,

from the breeze that was suddenly simpler,
as if there could once more be joy. It had been
months since I'd felt like myself, like Marie;
months since my life had moved for me.

KOURETES:

    is still thriving, making a silence

. . . It had been
months since I'd felt like myself, like Marie;
months since my life had moved for me.

LILY:

    deep in me still, a yielding mine,
    where my own thoughts cannot find a foothold
    but plummet, hopeless, down in my body,
    absorbed by its power. I stay quiet.
    Houses start to thin out around me.

    I didn't say anything, watching her shoulders
    as she finished picking, and raised herself, squinting
    at the sun stretching down on the garden.

KOURETES:

    Houses start to thin out around me.
    Night fills the horizon's undulations,
    branching out in darkening trees.

    "When my daughter Persephone was young," she said finally,
    "she cried every time I pulled weeds. It was hard

    to see that. It's hard to let go, but we need to."

LILY:

    We are approaching the Serpent Mound,

KOURETES:

    We are approaching the Serpent Mound
    We are approaching the Serpent Mound

We went inside quietly, washed off our hands,
and that night I slept in the bed in her barn,
where dreams of the animals nuzzled and licked me
through my long dreams. I woke up with a road,
a path, and a promise. Brigid stayed with Demeter;
I walked to the bus station, feet moving quietly
on the earth, the cement, and the asphalt,
eyes moving calm over trees, streetlights, buildings.

KOURETES:

    We are approaching the Serpent Mound

LILY:

    I walk cautiously, knowing my belly
    full of wide wings, night, and starlight.
    (*She approaches the house. A flame shines through a window.*)
    I can see her, sitting, sewing
    on a huge tapestry.

    LILY *knocks.*

BOOK 7: KALI

On the shaking and rattling bus
feeling nauseous, I looked for courage.
The other heart had begun its beating
in the rich cave, the long silence,
the hoping morning that had been my womb.
Through my belly ran knife-hard images
to my body and to my heart.
For the first time, the pregnancy hurt me.
I knew its life could betray mine soon.

The hate that had touched me on the mountain
was still thriving, making a silence
deep in me still, a yielding mine,
where my own thoughts could not find a foothold
but plummeted, hopeless, down in my body,
absorbed by its power. I stayed quiet.
Houses started to thin out around me.
Night filled the horizon's undulations,
branching out in darkening trees.

KOURETES:
    She stands up slowly.
    She puts the tapestry down on the table.

Then the bus stopped. Leaves brushed at the windows.
Rain was coming. I knew through the thick sky
the smell of water, along with dusk.
We were approaching the Serpent Mound,
where an ancient hill made a long grassy snake
coiling hard in the wilding night.
Rain pulled at me with the air of a distance
as the driver opened the door.
Soon I would get out and look for Kali.

With a rattle of strap and backpack,
missing Brigid, I moved to the door
and looked out while we rocked to a stop.
The dark highway led me from the others,
and then a narrow path led to Kali.
Mist soaked my skin, and the night finally entered.
Past the place where the edge of the Mound
was spiralling, I moved, through untrimmed branches
wet with rain, to her muddy driveway.

KOURETES:
　　She stands up slowly.
　　She puts the tapestry down on the table.
　　We see in its folds a glimpse of creation,
　　animals, planets, mountains, and trees,
　　embroidered thick with contrasts and colors,
　　on a background as warm as blood.

The door opens. KALI *appears there, looks around blankly, and shuts the door.*

I walked cautiously, knowing my belly
full of wide wings, night, and starlight.
Her small light shone like a flame through one window
where I could see her, sitting, sewing
on a huge tapestry. I knocked and waited
in the rain, as she stood up slowly
and carefully put it down on the table.
I saw in its folds a glimpse of creation,
animals, planets, mountains, and trees,

embroidered thick with contrasts and colors,
on a background as warm as blood.

After a moment of silence, LILY *runs forward angrily and pounds on the door.*

LILY (*pounding*):
>Kali! Kali! Come back out here!
>Let me in! Kali! Kali!

KALI, *who is very small, opens the door again and stands there staring at*
LILY. LILY *moves to stand beside her in the doorway.* KALI *suddenly brush-*
es past her resentfully. LILY *follows her in.*

Then she opened the door. I was nervous,
and drew back a moment, speechless, waiting
for her to see me. What would she do?
Nothing. All she did was stand there
one long minute, with hollow eyes
in a chiselled face, blind to my body,
look unfocussed, and shut the door.

Gouged and shocked, with those two sharp impressions
shadowing my eyes, where her smudged, sightless vision
had absorbed me, undone me, and left me
as wet as invisible, outside the door,
I half-panicked. I thought of leaving,
but then ran forward in desperate anger
and pounded again on the glistening wood,
shouting, calling, cursing and threatening her
till she finally answered, and focused, and stared.

She stared up and down and stared right through me,
half-attentive and clearly resentful,
while I stood on the doorstep. And then,
when I had followed her purposefully in
and stood beside her, towering past her,
I saw that her tiny face was resigned,
ready to help me. She grew taller,
it seemed, and harder, and I was confused
and drew far back so she could walk by.

SCENE 3.

Inside Kali's house. The huge tapestry rests on a table at stage left. There is a wall in the center of the stage with a cupboard, painted red with a purple border, and a door leading to another, smaller room which is in darkness so complete it is nearly impossible to see it.

KALI goes to a cupboard and takes out a tall jar filled with dried flowers. She takes out a handful and puts them in a bowl with something from another jar. She opens the door and urges Lily into the small room. LILY sits on the floor while KALI pounds and mixes up the contents of the bowl, opens the door again and puts the bowl on the floor. She gestures lily to drink. LILY drinks it slowly and puts the bowl down. KALI takes the bowl and leaves.

Did I have to explain what I wanted?
Did she wait till I tried to explain?
No, of course not; she'd known my story
before I had come. She was Kali;
she stretched now and reached into a cupboard,
painted red with a purple border,
pulled a bowl out, and scooped in something
from a tall jar—it looked like dried flowers,
Queen Anne's lace maybe, though it was crumbled—

—and gave it to me. While I held it, she rummaged,
found a jar and poured something else in,
mixed them, gestured me into a room,
closed the door, and left me there in darkness
which soon settled. Then I could see
a whole room full of motionless faces.
Each one was staring. She opened the door,
blinding me, brought in the bowl, and set it
on the floor by my feet, and gestured

for me to drink it. I drank it and coughed.
Before I had finished, she left me again.
In the light, I had seen a mattress,
cushion, and basin laid out on the floor,
and two walls that were full of statues
resting on shelves, mostly small, but one huge,
towering past me. I stared at her robes,
which I dimly saw now, as darkness
moved in closer for a long night's ordeal.

Scene 4.

The left side of the stage goes completely dark, and the room on the right is dimly lit to reveal at least a hundred different statues of goddesses on shelves around the room. One statue of Inanna at the back of the stage is much larger than the others. There are also a mattress, cushion, and basin on the floor.

KOURETES are on the left side of the stage. They begin to chant softly to the traditional tune: "Isis, Astarte, Diana, Hecate, Demeter, Kali—Inanna."

LILY coughs. She lies down to sleep and stirs restlessly.

KALI appears at the edge of the stage, addressing audience and Kouretes.

KALI:

    All night she half-slept,
    nauseous, scared, but not quite alone,
    listening to movement in her belly

KOURETES:

    staring into the room's huge night
     at her guardian, the hollow-eyed giant

KALI AND KOURETES:

    called Inanna, with robes like the sky.

LILY (*sitting up*):

    She looks right at me
    with eyes that swallow. Hours and hours
    of darkness fall into her eyes.

KOURETES:

    Inanna, Inanna, Inanna, Inanna
    Inanna, Inanna, Inanna, Inanna

KALI:

    Then it was morning; she must have slept, finally.

KOURETES:

    Dawn pressed hard at her through the trees.
    Dawn pressed hard at her through the trees.

LILY (*going to the door*):

    I am more nauseous, not even hungry.

    She pushes at the door, then paces.

KOURETES:

    the door was locked, and the house stayed quiet
    all day.

LILY (*pacing*):
    I don't even think she is there.

Lying down, I knew I would stay there
with the eyes of the centuries on me
longer than a century. All night I half-slept,
nauseous, scared, but not quite alone,
listening to movement in my belly,
reaching constantly with my eyes,
staring into the room's huge night
at my guardian, the hollow-eyed giant
called Inanna, with robes like the sky.

    LILY *goes over to look at the statues.*

LILY:
    so my hunger and sickness kept me . . .

KOURETES:
    two more nights, and three more days

LILY:
    weak but wakeful. I could see them . . .

In the darkness, she looked right at me
with eyes that swallowed. Hours' and hours'
worth of darkness fell into her eyes.
I could tell it was she, from the bulls' horns
that surmounted her face like the moon,
and the fearless concentration
she stood still with—her towering focus.

KOURETES:
    two more nights, and three more days

LILY:
    They can see me!

They can see me!

KOURETES:
    dozens, watching her with eyes,
    squatting goddesses, with children or alone,
    alabaster, or dark burned stone,
    mouths sometimes open, sometimes in pain,
    chipped out hollows shadowing distance,
    inset eyes of turquoise staring

KALI:
    And the queen of heaven, Inanna,
    never left her eyes alone;

LILY (*standing center stage to face audience*):
    hard on the beams of her eyes I went downward
    (*She falls to the floor, raises herself on one arm.*)
    till that day passed, and evening came,
    and into the second night's solitude

KALI:
    there rose another, terrible Queen.

Then it was morning; I guess I'd slept, finally.
Dawn pressed hard at me through the trees.

I was more nauseous, not even hungry,
but I stood up and pushed at the door,
wanting distraction. There were no distractions;
the door was locked, and the house stayed quiet
all day. I don't even think she was there.
So those statues were my companions
two more nights, and three more days,
as my hunger and sickness kept me
weak but wakeful. I could see them,

dozens, watching me with eyes,
squatting goddesses, with children or alone,
alabaster, or dark burned stone,
mouths sometimes open, sometimes in pain,
chipped out hollows shadowing distance,
inset eyes of turquoise staring
from attenuated heights.
And the queen of heaven, Inanna,
never left my eyes alone;

hard on the beams of her eyes I went downward
till that day passed, and evening came,
and into the second night's solitude
there rose another, terrible Queen.

LILY (*as* KALI *mimes the actions of the Queen Ereshkigal*):
    She stood over me with the height of a murderer,
    her hand on my belly, her voice in my blood,

KALI (*as* LILY *lies down*):
    Ereshkigel, Ereshkigel

KOURETES:
    while Inanna watched without one movement.

LILY (*rising to her knees*):
    Till the dawn came, I felt that hand
    burning, and I knew the flame

She stood over me with the height of a murderer,
her hand on my belly, her voice in my blood,
while Inanna watched me without one movement.
Till the dawn came, I felt that hand
burning, and I knew the flame

KALI:
    was spinning, heavy, out from her forehead,

resting between my eyes like new wisdom,
as my pregnancy shrank and contracted.
Inanna had taken me to the vision,
and she held me there till it was over,
under Ereshkigal's hand. They all saw me
as death moved through me, and I took a life,
so many of them, without pity or fear,
massed on the shelves with their eyes wide open.

LILY (*rising*):
    as death moved through me, and I took a life,

as my pregnancy shrank and contracted.

KOURETES:
    as death moved through her, and she took a life

Inanna had taken me to the vision,
and she held me there till it was over,

KALI:
    as death moved through her, and she took a life

as my pregnancy shrank and contracted.
Inanna had taken me to the vision,
and she held me there till it was over,
under Ereshkigal's hand. They all saw me
as death moved through me, and I took a life,
so many of them, without pity or fear,
massed on the shelves with their eyes wide open.

KALI AND KOURETES (*to the traditional tune*):
    Isis, Astarte, Diana, Hecate, Demeter, Kali, Inanna...
    Death moved through her, and she took a life
    Death moved through her, and she took a life

KALI (*slowly opening the door and going to stand with* LILY, *then speaking, not singing*):
    She waited till evening,
    with Inanna's eyes on her, steady
    as the sun she ruled ruled the day.

KOURETES:
    Death moved through her, and she took a life

LILY:
    All I wanted was there

KALI AND LILY:
    day and its lover, night and its lover

KALI:
    brought by Inanna.

LILY:
    They healed the pain.

KOURETES:
    In the gray light, she left the room.

    LILY *moves offstage.*

    End of Act III.

By the third morning, weak and thirsty,
no longer nauseous, I lay in a daze,
waiting for Kali. I waited till evening,
with Inanna's eyes on me, steady
as the sun she ruled ruled the day,
and stopped at dusk. All I wanted was there,
day and its lover, night and its lover,
brought by Inanna. They healed the pain.
In the gray light, I left the room.

83

EPILOGUE

Many years later. In colored light that dapples the stage like light through stained glass, LILY *and a circle of other older women, a few young women, and two or three children are gathered.* LILY *is holding her young baby. At the back of the stage is the silhouette of a very old tree with a few leaves.*

CIRCLE OF WOMEN:
    Gathering women who touch, who honor,
    who loom traditions through the body of earth,
    Here is the end that is made of beginnings.
    gathering women who touch, who honor,
    who loom traditions through the body of earth.

A crescent moon rises slowly through the branches of the tree as they weave and dance.

WOMEN:
    The moon! The moon!

CHILDREN (*crowding around* LILY *and the baby*):
    Show the baby the moon, Lily! Show the baby!

LILY (*to her baby*):
    Look, Eve, it's the moon!

WOMEN:
    Here is the end that is made of beginnings.

End.

APPENDIX

AN AFTER-ABORTION RITUAL FOR RECOVERY AND HEALING

This ritual can be done alone or with any or all members of the family or community affected by the abortion.

PREPARATION

Prepare for the ritual ahead of time by taking quiet time to write a letter to the baby. Young children, or those who prefer not to write, may draw a picture for the baby, or create a piece of music or a dance. Bring along some grain such as millet, rice, oats, or flour. Also think about how you will give the four elements to the baby, and which chant or song you would like to sing.

THE RITUAL

Build a small circular altar of sticks piled as high as you like. Put anything you like on top: a shell, grass, special objects.

Arrange yourselves around the altar. If a family does the ritual together, the parents might want to stand in the north and south.

Create a sacred space around the altar. This can be done by calling in the directions to cast a circle, or in any way you like. To call in the directions simply, face each compass direction and ask "spirits of the east (south, west, north), please be with us."

Call in any ancestors or spiritual guides or presences whose company or support you would like.

Say hello to the spirit of the baby. Each person should use a name that feels right to them; the names can be all the same or different.

Convey your messages to the baby aloud. Read letters, talk about pictures, and perform any music or dance messages.

Add the four elements to the altar: Earth (perhaps a special rock or stone), air (your letters or pictures, or a feather), water (a little can be poured on the altar or left in a receptacle) and fire (a crystal is good for this).

Choose a simple song, such as "The earth, the air, the fire, the water, re-turn, return, return, return." (This is a common chant and the tune is available online at youtube and elsewhere). If you are in a group, sing it together standing still, then in a round (perhaps with female/male parts or however you want to break it up), then together again while holding hands and circling the altar (counterclockwise for releasing).

Scatter grain around the area to symbolize the life-force (or goddess or god) who gave the baby life, gave each of us to our parents, and is the source of life. You can sing another song together while doing this (a child in our family chose "Happy Birthday.")

Tell the baby goodbye, thank you, and that it will always be a part of your family.

Open (disband) the circle by reversing whatever you did to cast it. Say thank you and goodbye to any ancestors or spirits you invoked.

Be sure to allow some quiet time together afterwards to absorb the ritual.

BIOGRAPHICAL NOTE

Annie Finch is the author of four books of poetry, *Eve, Calendars* (a finalist for the Forward Poetry Book of the Year Award), *The Encyclopedia of Scotland* (Salt Publishing), and *Among the Goddesses: An Epic and Libretto* (Red Hen Press). Annie's book of poetry *Calendars* was short-listed for the Foreword Poetry Book of the Year Award and in 2009 she was awarded the Robert Fitzgerald Award. She has performed her poetry across the U.S. and in England, France, Greece, Ireland, and Spain. Annie lives on the Maine coast near Portland where she directs Stonecoast, the low-residency MFA program in creative writing at the University of Southern Maine.